Swipe, Sip, and Surrender:

One Woman's Journey of Dating in Her Fifties

Sydney Allison

First Edition published by Mind and Power, Inc. 2025

ISBN: 979-8-9994231-0-8

.

Prologue

I never imagined myself at 58 years old, single, and, dare I say, thriving. Yet, here I am, embracing a season of life that feels refreshingly liberating. For the first time, I am not chasing love or partnership. I am simply being. I have come to understand that dating might just not be my journey, and honestly, I am okay with that. Celibacy suits me, and through this journey, I‘ve realized the spiritual weight intimacy carries. Each connection we form leaves a thread, a spiritual tether that isn't easy to sever. And frankly? Dating today feels like navigating a minefield. The games, the uncertainty, the unspoken truths. It is just more than I want to deal with.

I’ve grown weary of the effort it takes to vet someone’s intentions or sort through red flags. Will they match my stride, whether financially, emotionally, or spiritually? Will they be trustworthy or bring along hidden baggage, substance abuse, legal troubles, or worse? And let’s not even talk about the "smaller" things like living with their mother or lacking basic independence. Ladies, if you can relate, this book is for you.

These stories, some true, some not, with names changed to protect the guilty are my gift to you. Let’s laugh, cry, and commiserate together because, in this phase of life, who has time for anything less than the truth?

Seriously Though?

My girlfriends and I have a tradition of getting together at least once a week to unwind. Usually, it's at a local bar or restaurant, especially during the lively summer months. One evening, Kendra recommended a new bar she'd discovered online. The photos promised elegance, an older crowd in their 50s, and a "sexy" ambiance. Naturally, we were curious. What else did we have to do? All in our late 50s, single, and enjoying empty nests, we were eager to explore.

We arrived together and were immediately struck by the place's charm. The air was perfumed with a rainforest mist that made the atmosphere almost intoxicating. As we stood soaking it all in, I caught the gaze of a tall, striking man across the room. His intensity lingered, but I refused to let my curiosity show.

While my friends found seats, I excused myself to the ladies' room. On my way out, there he was, 6’4" of impeccably dressed confidence. His black tailored suit and open white shirt revealed a black time necklace,

Louis Vuitton belt and loafers that screamed sophistication. Even his Omega watch and black diamond bracelet whispered luxury. He introduced himself as Grant, his voice a melody of charm, and I couldn’t help but notice the orchestra he composed—head to toe.

Grant offered to buy me a drink, to which I agreed, and we found ourselves immersed in conversation at one of the many large booths, in a cubby on the main floor of the

establishment. He was magnetic, the kind of man who makes you wonder how the universe orchestrated your paths to cross. After two hours of easy, flowing conversation in that cozy nook, I realized how late it had gotten—1 a.m. With an early morning of clients awaiting me. I thanked him for the evening, and he walked me to my car, where he asked for my number. His kiss goodbye was in the air, but the charm stayed with me. He asked me to text him when I got home to ensure I made it home safely.

Arriving home, I removed my makeup, slipped into comfort, and texted him as promised. His reply was instant and warm, yet I reminded myself not to get carried away. I'd learned the hard way that hope, paired with expectations, often ends in disappointment. The tarot readings, the giddy post-date fantasies, they'd all led me to heartbreaks wrapped in red flags. This time, I'd approach with caution and curiosity, nothing more.

Grant proved himself to be remarkably consistent, maintaining daily conversations with me even amidst his busy schedule. Just a few days after our first encounter, he embarked on a two-week business trip to visit some clients. As a life coach with a thriving business, his achievements mirrored my own profession as an executive coach. The shared connection deepened our bond. Despite the distance, he made a point to keep in touch, ensuring that our budding relationship remained strong.

Over time, I found myself lowering my defenses, allowing a sense of trust to grow. When Grant returned from his trip, he invited me to join him for dinner and drinks in downtown Chicago, and I eagerly accepted. Opting for the convenience of the Metra, I made my way to Ocean Prime—a restaurant just a short walk from the station. Grant greeted me with a presence that was nothing short of captivating.

Dressed impeccably in a Versace shirt, complemented by a black diamond necklace, a matching Versace belt, sleek black pants, and stylish Versace loafers, he embodied sophistication and confidence. His undeniable swag was impossible to ignore, making the evening one to remember as I couldn't keep my eyes off him.

Although we talked several times a day, we were never at a loss for words. Our conversations spanned a wide array of topics—from childhood memories to professional ambitions, favorite travel destinations, and even thoughts on life's deeper mysteries were never forced or dull. Each exchange felt like a dance, where the rhythm was set by mutual curiosity and respect. Whether sharing a laugh over a silly anecdote or diving into profound topics about personal growth and resilience, our connection seemed effortless, a rare blend of intellectual stimulation and emotional resonance. It was as if we were discovering new dimensions of each other with every passing day.

Grant respected the space between us, refraining from holding my hand or leaning in for a kiss in that intimate booth. It was a gesture I deeply valued, revealing his understanding of boundaries even as we continued to connect after three weeks of conversations. As the evening ended, he settled the bill and then asked, with considerate precision, if I would like a ride to the train station where I had parked my car. His thoughtfulness warmed me, and I eagerly accepted, not quite ready for the night to end.

We strolled toward his car, the conversation still flowing effortlessly, and as we approached, I was struck by a vision of elegance, a white Porsche Panamera, its top down, gleaming in the soft city lights in front of a luxury condo and office building. It was a moment of surprise that encapsulated the sophistication and charm Grant carried with him, leaving me curious about the layers yet to be unveiled.

Over the course of three months, Grant and I enjoyed a series of delightful outings. We explored the Art Museum, swayed to jazz at the Shedd, strolled along Navy Pier, and immersed ourselves in the exhibits at the Chicago History Museum. Our adventures also led us to a variety of restaurants and bars, each visit adding new layers to our connection. As I spent more time with him, I discovered more about who he was, deepening my appreciation for his company. Then, one evening after a lovely date, he walked me to my door. As he leaned in for a kiss, I didn't turn away. That kiss, our first, was everything I hadn't expected yet somehow everything I hoped it would be. Until that moment, our physical contact had been limited to small, thoughtful gestures—holding my hand as he guided me across the street or his arm resting lightly around my waist as he escorted me into a building. This, however, was a new beginning.

While I found myself increasingly drawn to him, a lingering apprehension held me back from becoming too vulnerable. Past experiences had taught me the pain of lowering my defenses too quickly, and I was determined not to repeat those mistakes. Even after four months, our relationship had not become physical, a boundary I appreciated and one he respected without pressure. He exuded an irresistible allure, a magnetism that made it challenging to remain unaffected by his presence. To navigate these emotions with grace, I self-pleasured to steady myself before our dates, ensuring I could approach the evening with composure and clarity.

Since I love to entertain, I decided to host a small friends and family gathering at my home. The guest list was intimate, just close friends and a few acquaintances. Of course, I invited Grant, as we were still enjoying the early, platonic stages of getting to know each other. I was in the kitchen when he arrived, but when I saw him, he was sharp as ever, carrying a bag with a change of clothes for an event he planned to attend later. I told him that he could place his things in my room and escorted him there as he had never been inside my home before. I had learned the hard way not to allow a man in my house unless I was having a gathering. It seemed that when I allowed a Netflix and chill date, that became the norm. So, I stayed away from that.

The evening was lively, friends arriving and conversation flowing. At one point, Grant went to my bedroom to change into the attire he brought. I followed shortly after to check in, only to be joined by one of my girlfriends who had been mid-conversation with me. As Grant emerged from the bathroom, she greeted him in a way that made my stomach twist. “Oh, you’re ready to go,” she said casually. I froze, piecing the puzzle together, and asked her outright if they were involved. Her reply? A nonchalant "Yes." My heart sank as I turned to Grant, and asked him if he knew we were friends? He offered nothing but a weak "Well" in response. It seemed impossible that he wouldn’t have realized during their interactions that they were both planning to attend the same gathering at my house.

Seriously though? I escorted them both to the door, my composure unwavering despite the sting of betrayal. As they walked toward his car, the realization struck me—it was clear they had arrived together. How could Grant bring another date to an event hosted by someone he was actively courting? The sheer audacity and lack of respect left me speechless, a sharp reminder of the disregard for boundaries and decency I had so often experienced in the past.

By this time the house was crowded with guests—friends of friends I didn't even know. I shrugged to myself, thinking, "No worries. Plenty of new faces. Time to move on to the next chapter." I never heard from him again. No explanation.

I'm deeply grateful that we never shared physical intimacy; such an act would have amplified emotions, making it far more challenging to move forward.

Dating in your 50s is a rollercoaster of emotions, surprises, and lessons. It's not about finding "the one" anymore; it's about finding yourself amid the chaos. Swipe, sip, and surrender, because life is too short not to embrace the adventure.

Summer Breeze

In the quiet of the night, when the world is still, I find myself reflecting, feeling the chill. You were a chapter, a story untold, a journey of emotions, both young and old.

You came into my life like a summer breeze, with promises of forever, and moments to seize. But as the seasons changed, so did we, and the love we once had, was no longer free.

The pain was deep, like a wound unhealed, but time, they say, has a way to reveal. The strength within, the courage to mend, to find the light, around the bend.

I cried rivers, I screamed to the skies, questioning the reasons, the where's and whys. But in the midst of sorrow, I found my grace, A resilience within, a new embrace.

Healing isn't linear, it's a winding road, with ups and downs, a heavy load. But each step forward, no matter how small, is a victory, a rise after the fall.

You were a lesson, a moment in time, a part of my story, a rhythm, a rhyme. And though we parted, and went our ways, I thank you for the growth, the brighter days.

For in the ashes of what once was, I found myself, my purpose, my cause. To love again, to trust, to be free, to embrace the person, I was meant to be.

Like a seed in the soil, buried and unseen, I grew roots of strength, and leaves of green. Through the storms and the rain, I stood tall, blossoming anew, after the fall.

So, here's to healing, to moving on, to finding peace, when the pain is gone. You were a chapter, but not the end, for in own my heart, I found a friend.

Ignoring Red Flags

I opened my dresser drawer to find something to sleep in and realized that I had a plethora of nighties that still had the tag on them. It made me recall why I purchased them. Here's the story. On January 9th, Phi Beta Sigma Founder's Day, I was reflecting on a recent breakup that had occurred in December after four months of dating. With this in mind, I decided to reach out to one of my favorite Sigma brothers to inquire about his plans for the evening. He informed me that the Sigma's were hosting a Founder's Day celebration at an event space in the city; however, he would not be attending due to other commitments.

As I continued with my day, completing errands and getting my nails done, I felt compelled to attend the celebration. Initially, I hesitated but ultimately reasoned that it would be a worthwhile experience, given I had no other plans. I checked online for ticket availability, purchased one, and then returned home to prepare. I showered, dressed in a black top and pants, added a fedora, and informed my son's nurse of my intention to meet my "Sigma" husband.

As a member of Zeta Phi Beta, we hold a unique constitutional bond with Phi Beta Sigma, making us the only organizations within the Divine Nine with a fraternal constitutionally binding relationship. This connection, often referred to as the "blue and white family," is a source of pride and aspiration for many Zetas who wish to marry a Sigma, creating the ideal of a "blue and white wedding." Personally, I have also cherished this vision, including the symbolism of a blue sapphire and diamond ring and the involvement of both Zetas and Sigma's in traditional wedding activities.

I was eager to attend the event, and upon arrival, I noted that the parking lot was quite full, which suggested a significant turnout. However, once inside, I discovered ample seating was available. I approached the bar, engaged in conversation with familiar sorority sisters (other Zetas) and Sigma members, before finding myself a seat.

I sat alone for quite some time before texting another Sigma brother to inquire if he and his ship would be in attendance. He informed me that he was already in the building by the bar, and I courteously proceeded to locate him. It had been years since our last encounter, and I was delighted to be in their company once again. After greeting each other, we sought out some seats. However, before finding any, they encountered three other fraternity brothers and one soror. They greeted each other and introduced me. Jean, a frat that I was just introduced to complemented me on my hat and I joined a quick group photo with all seven of us. Suddenly, four people left, leaving Gray, Jean, and me. Gray and I then had a conversation, and before long, Jean also left. I enjoyed talking with Gray and he asked me for my phone number. I obliged but knew that he was not my type. I excused myself and bumped into a frat I had a crush on for years, Trenton. We reintroduced ourselves; he didn't remember me as I'd lost weight and looked different since the Chosen Few picnic. He was seeing someone else but was still attractive. He bought me a drink, we exchanged numbers, and he returned to his security job. He asked me to see him before he left.

The Sigmas formed a circle singing their fraternity song, which was impressive. Before leaving, I walked around the venue again and stood next to Jean. Seeing him up close, I noticed he was handsome, well-dressed in a dress shirt and slacks, with a black fedora, trimmed beard, and a beautiful smile.

I told him that I was about to go and it was nice

meeting him. He told he that same and said: "Hopefully, we'll see each other again". That was my cue, I was fast on my feet and asked him: 'And how to you plan on doing that?" He responded: "Oh, well then, what's your number?" We exchanged phone numbers, and I headed for the door. Before leaving I ran back into my crush, Trenton. He gave me a hug and told me to text him when I made it home.

When I got home, I texted both Trenton and Jean. Jean replied quickly and called me 20 minutes later. We talked for about an hour before Trenton called, and I asked Jean if I could call him back. Trenton and I chatted briefly, then I resumed my conversation with Jean for another two hours. Jean intrigued me; despite being 66 years old, he didn't look it. Younger guys seemed to be my preference. He was retired with two adult sons and a teenage granddaughter. We began talking daily and developed a nice rapport, discussing everything. We planned to meet the following week, but I fell sick and we continued our lengthy conversations daily.

Once I recovered, Jean invited me over. It would be our first time seeing each other since we met. He lived about 45 minutes away, but I simply listened to my Apple playlist. I felt comfortable going to his house because of the trust we had built from the long daily conversations we had over the previous weeks. We would talk perhaps 2-3 times a day no less than 1 hour each time. When I got to his house, he eagerly opened the door, gave me a hug and took my coat.

His home was immaculate. One would have sworn that a woman lived there. I mean it was clean. He escorted me back into his family room and we sat on the couch. A few minutes later he decided to take me on a tour. His place was phenomenal. I couldn't help but think about the cleaning I needed to do, if I were to ever invite him over. After the tour, we sat back on the couch, and he held and caressed my hand. Then, it happened. That first kiss. He was a great kisser. I couldn't believe that it was so good, I found myself getting a little moist, if you know what I mean. The kiss led to an all-out make-out session. I had said to myself and to him that he was not going to get any but before I knew it, I could feel his bulge, and I was ready for it. He politely led me to his bedroom, and we took off our clothes. We laid across the bed. Then he got up and retrieved a condom from his nightstand. Damnit, I was ready. Those kisses continued and got wetter. The time had come for him to enter my box. I could not even remember when I wanted someone that bad or when my pussy was that wet. As I laid on my back, he raised up a little to put that dick in. There was a struggle. He had gone down. He couldn't get it back up. He looked like he was in shear panic. He kept trying and trying to no avail. What the fuck? I was in horror. I gently rolled over and gave him head and that didn't even work. But he did what good lovers do, went down on me. He licked and kissed and licked and kissed until that pussy came! He was satisfied that I was satisfied. It was amazing.

We got up and took showers in separate bathrooms. He then surprised me by cooking us a meal, salmon, salad, and portobello mushrooms. It was his first time cooking portobellos but he refused to allow me to assist. Dinner was great. He was a good cook. When it was time to clear the table, he wouldn't allow me to. I watched as he meticulously cleaned the dishes, counters, and table. Then, he dried the dishes and pans and put them away. I was not surprised because he was a Virgo and I didn't expect any other type of behavior. We went back into the family room, and he began holding my hand again. He was so embarrassed. He couldn't stop talking about our sexual interaction and his inability to perform. I kept reassuring him that it was okay. But he continued to beat himself up about it. After about an hour, it was time for me to leave. So, he walked me to the door, grabbed my coat, helped me put it on and watched me to my car. I called him when I made it home. We talked for a couple of hours and then got off the phone to go to bed. The next day we talked our regular 3 hours, and he said he was feeling ill. We were supposed to see each other the upcoming weekend, but now he was sick. We talked on the phone the whole time he was sick. Two weeks later we were able to reconnect. I drove back to his house.

In his mind, this was his opportunity to make up for the debacle that happened the first time we got together. And truthfully, I so did I. We started out with general small talk. You know, the regular how are you doing today? What's been going on? Although, we already knew the answer to those questions. Then, we got to making out. Next, was that offer to go to his room. I had added him as a family member to my Apple account, so he had access to my iTunes library. So, he unplugged the Bluetooth speaker that was in the living room and brought it to his bedroom, plugged it back up and immediately went to the playlist and we generally listen to when I came out to his house. I take off my clothes. He takes off his clothes and now we get the opportunity to try again, but this time it was different. He was able to maintain and keep a hard on, and it was good. He went down on me, and it was phenomenal. And then he came. Once we got done, I went to the guest bathroom to take a shower. He went to his room to take a shower.

The funny thing about it is the first thing that came to my mind was that he must've taken a little blue pill. And maybe that's why he had erectile dysfunction the first time because he hadn't taken the little blue pill. He probably had no expectation that we very well might have sex. He clearly went in his bottom drawer again before we started and retrieved the condom, so he keeps them on board. Which means that he's prepared. Or he's been having sex with somebody. Nevertheless, we ended up ordering a pizza from a nearby restaurant. I drove and picked it up and we brought it back to his house to eat. Still no official date. Earlier on when we were officially getting to know each other and asking each other a lot of questions. He asked me what my favorite restaurants were. Most of them are in Streeterville. I also like Ruth Chris, which is in Oak Brook now. What was funny was there was no mention of us going to any of my favorite restaurants that he's so vehemently said that he wanted to take me to. But even with this being the case, I felt like we were on the same level. I felt like there was something organic between us. He was someone that showed interest in spending time with me by the long phone calls every day after work. And the desire to spend time with me on the weekends. What was interesting though there was no plan ever for us to do anything outside of his house.

One day I was talking to my sister, Talithia, and she asked me if we have been out yet. Of course, I told her "no". And she began to kind of shake my nervous system. She asked, "why not." I think I was embarrassed because I had allowed him to have my body, and he hadn't proven anything to me as it pertains to his true care concern and desire to treat me as a woman should be treated. A lot of things started to bubble up for me at that point. I started to think about the things that we discussed in retrospect. I remember us discussing his sons. And he said they were both by the same mother. But when I asked him how long they were married, he said he couldn't remember. He stated that he just wasn't good with anniversaries or birthdays, he just didn't seem to remember those types of things, so they weren't very important to him as they pertained to her at this stage since they were divorced. I kept attempting to piece together the timeline of his marriages and the ages of his sons, but I was consistently incorrect.

This is likely when I began to notice some warning signs. I also remember him telling me a story about a lady that he was dating who he had met through a friend at an AKA event and he had gotten her phone number. He said that he had taken her out for dinner and she ordered a lot of food. She only dabbled in the food a little bit and then she asked for a to-go container, but she also asked for dessert. That really got under his skin. He also stated that he didn't see her for two weeks when they first met and to him that showed that she wasn't that interested. But, after that incident he still took her to dinner. He felt used when she ordered excessive food but left it untouched. So, he just simply stopped talking to her. He ghosted her. Cut her right off. Just complete abandonment. When he first shared that story with me, I could see why he disapproved of her behavior, but I didn't think it was enough to end a relationship or even one just beginning over a single incident.

Actually, it gave me pause. As I reflected on our conversation, I noticed even more red flags than I'd like to admit. The next date was at my house. He brought me roses and candy for Valentine's Day. By this time, we were exclusive. He mentioned his car's tires were bald, but that barely captured how worn they really were. He had meant to get them fixed the week before, but previously mentioned his bank account was robbed of $6000 and he was trying to recover it. I assumed he might have experienced some financial difficulties after retiring and the loss of the money from his account. But he drove it anyway to come and see me even during a snowstorm. When we looked out the window and realized that the snow was coming down like a white wall, he decided he should leave. I asked him to stay because the weather was so bad, and tires on his car were "bald". But he insisted that he must go anyway, and that he would call me when he got home. He called about 30 minutes later to say he was near the oasis on the tollway and would head to his cousin's house until the snow eased. About an hour later, he called to say he was home. He'd only stayed at his cousin's house for 15 minutes because the atmosphere made him uncomfortable, so he left and took his chances getting home.

I thought nothing of it at the time until I spoke to my sister again. And she said her spirit told her that he could be a player. She felt like he had to leave so abruptly because maybe he needed to drop off roses and candy at someone else's house as well. That sat with me for a minute, and of course I didn't have any proof that this may be the case. So, I just kept it in my mental Rolodex.

There were several red flags I should've questioned and noticed in his behavior. The next time we got together was at my house this time. He had been over before but hadn't stayed long because he had a long drive back home. We still had not gone on an official date. We had gotten into this cadence of either him coming over my house, listening to music and having sex or me going to his and doing the same. I mentioned to him one day that I wanted him to spend the night. So, the next time he came over, he did. It was nice waking up to him in the morning and having that good morning love.

One night, when we were talking on the phone, he told me he had to call me back because his mother was calling on the other line. I was so exhausted that I fell asleep. Earlier that day, I silenced my phone at work and forgot to turn the ringer back on. When I finally talked to him after work the next day, he was furious. We got into disagreement because I didn't answer when he called. The conversation made me feel bad. I couldn't believe he was upset. He made mention of not playing games and asked me how I would feel if he didn't answer when I called him back. His comments made me uneasy and triggered my abandonment issues. He said he only contacted me because I called but decided to let it go since he liked me. I recalled the previous conversations about his dating experiences and how he so easily walked away. I believe this is the first time

I started to really feel unsafe and this relationship. I printed our photos as 8x10s at Walgreens, framed them in my room. I took our relationship seriously. It had been the first time in a long time that I have met someone who was financially independent, we shared so many of the same desires and likes, he seemed to get my quirks, I had started to become vulnerable and letting my guard down because I felt like this could really be something. I can admit I had not started falling in love with him, but it had potential. I was willing to take the risk to see. And he was mad at me because I was asleep when he called me back. He knew I had a special needs son and often didn't get a lot of sleep. Was he suggesting I was seeing someone else, despite our agreement to be monogamous? It really left me scratching my head. Finally, the heat calmed down after I apologized for being asleep when he called me back. Another big red flag for a few reasons. To begin with, he shouldn't have gotten upset over something so trivial and I shouldn't have apologized for his emotional problems. But I did so to keep the peace and to see where this relationship could go.

We got back on track and I was back to being excited about "my man, my man, my man." On occasion, I would get nursing on a Friday evening, and it is a treat. On this particular evening, my girlfriend was having a birthday party. I spoke with Jean at 4pm, which was earlier than usual. He had decided to return to work. He was required to be in the office three days a week, but on this day, he decided to leave early. I was back and forth on my decision to go to my girlfriend's party. He asked me a few times if I was going but I kept saying, "no." After our phone conversation, I thought, why not go? There will be Fridays when nursing isn't available, so I should take advantage of the opportunity while it's possible. So, I jumped up, threw on some clothes and headed to the party. I left fairly quickly since I wanted to visit my usual hangout. While I was there, Jean called. I picked up and told him I was out; he just replied, "Okay, I'll talk to you later." So, I ended the call. On the way home I called him, but he didn’t answer. I assumed he was unavailable at that time.

Therefore, I contacted him the following day while enroute to my nail appointment. He answered and was pissed. He informed me that my decision to go out without notifying him was considered deceptive. He pointed out that I had previously said I wouldn’t go out, implying my actions weren’t trustworthy. His anger caught me off guard once more. We hadn't planned to meet or talk that night, but he was very upset. He had disclosed in earlier conversations that he had anger issues, which I thought were resolved, but were obviously not based on what he was saying. I couldn’t believe we were here again with his anger about something so small from my perspective. We discussed it and basically agreed to disagree, but I did apologize for not letting him know that I had changed my mind.

By the next weekend, I was back at his house again but this time I played it a little differently. I told him that I wanted to go out and do something, I wanted to go to the movies. So, I went to his house, went straight to his bedroom, and took off my clothes so we could go ahead and have sex because I knew that's what he wanted. And truthfully, I did too. We made love and got up and took shower together. I noted to him that I found it somewhat unusual that after each intimate encounter, he would choose to use one shower while I used another, rather than us sharing the same shower together. He obliged me. In the meantime, the night before I had mentioned that I wanted his best friend to meet my niece and I thought that would be a good match. I had retrieved some pictures from her, the ones she wanted to send to him for his best friend and vice versa so she could see what he looked like. They were both down for the meeting. On the way to the theatre, he called his best friend and told him we were going to stop by after the movies because I wanted to show him some pictures of my niece. He was excited. I was excited too because we were finally doing something together. It was our first official date, and we had been seeing each other for two months. The time spent with him was great. He was such a gentleman. I thought to myself, "I could get used to this treatment." After the show we took the drive to his bestie's house. They were so funny together, just cracking jokes on each other. I enjoyed seeing them together and thought to myself that if his best friend and my niece got together, it would be fun for the four of us to hang out together. When I showed Malik the pictures he was enamored. I called Paige, my niece, while we were at Malik's house and gave him the phone so they could talk. They exchanged numbers and soon after Jean and I left. I dropped him off back at home and continued home to relieve my son's nurse. I called Paige as soon as I drove away from Jean's house and she wanted to know all of the details of Malik's house and his facial expression when he saw her picture.

The next day, Saturday, she stopped over at my house and we had a few drinks. She was so giddy. She had talked to Malik for three hours! She said the conversation was amazing. They had so much in common and were going to meet someday in the coming week. Jean and I were so excited for them. Jean told me later that evening how excited Malik was to make Paige's acquaintance. I was happy for Jean and I and Malik and Paige.

By Monday, Paige had not heard from Malik. She called me very upset because she didn't know what she could have done wrong. I called Jean and he said that he was mad at Malik for ghosting Paige. That was a bitch move. She was out Sunday when he called her, and she told him she would call him back. But when she called him back, he didn't answer and continued not to answer.

By Tuesday, Paige was highly upset. I continued to talk to Jean, but he had no answers to why this was happening. He said he had told Malik to at least call Paige and tell her something. Thursday, Paige and I talked for about 2 hours on the phone about the situation. She texted me later on and asked me if I was going to hang out that night and it was funny because I was going to call her and ask her the same question. So, we decided to meet up and our hang-out spot. I got there a little earlier and she arrived about an hour later. We were wondering what had happened that she was taking so long, and she said she was fixing her hair. We had such a great time that night, laughing and singing with the owner of the bar's mother, Darlene. It was the first time we had ever interacted with Darlene like that although Paige worked there sometimes and I had seen her many times before. I left around 9p so I could relieve my son's nurse, called Jean and said goodnight. At about 10:30p Paige called me to tell me how drunk another friend of ours was that night, but I didn't answer so she texted me. I didn't respond until about 3:00a. She didn't respond, so I figured she was asleep and would see the text in the morning. At 5a, Paige's oldest sister called me from Ohio. I answered the phone, and she told me that Paige had run into a tree the night before and had no brain activity! My heart instantly broke. I immediately called Jean. He couldn't believe it. They had Paige on life support for about a week and when her son came home from overseas, he made the decision to take her off. Jean was so supportive through this hard time for me. The family decided to have the funeral on my son's 18th birthday. I had so many mixed feelings. I knew I wasn't going to attend the services because I just couldn't handle it. Jean asked me every day if I was going and kept telling him that I wasn't. The Friday before the funeral he came over. He received a call from his sister that they needed to take his mother to the emergency room. His mother had cancer. He called me a few times while at the hospital and when he was about to leave he asked if he could come over. I was happy to see him. When I hung up his coat like usual, I noticed he hadn't removed his phone from his pocket. So, I asked him if he wanted it and he said that he did not. So, I left it alone but thought it was peculiar. He had just dropped his mother off back at home from an emergency room visit, yet didn't want his phone nearby in case there was another emergency with her? We went straight into my bedroom and had sex. Then we fell asleep. Something felt off. I woke up early to care for my son and left Jean in bed. Once I was done with my son, I got back in bed and Jean was already woke. We messed around again, and he got up and took a shower. I asked him if we were alright and he said we were. I felt uneasy. Like my gut was telling me that we were not okay.

Later that day, I watched the funeral of my niece and best friend. It was also my son's 18th birthday. I didn't know whether I should be happy or sad. IT HURT! My family came over to my house after the repast and hung out until 1am. I got up early the next day because I was having a birthday party for my son at his father's house. The party was nice although we were grieving. I called Jean when I got home, and we talked briefly about the day. I went to work Monday and talked to Jean when I got home as usual. He abruptly ended the call, saying his mother was calling and he'd call me back. He called me back and again said he needed to pick up some things for her from Costco. He was taking her to the doctor in the morning and wanted to already have the items in his vehicle. I was so very tired, I fell asleep. I was exhausted mentally, spiritually, emotionally, and physically. Jean called me at 10p, but I didn't hear the ringer. He texted me in all caps: "WHATS UP SYDNEY! WHY AREN'T

YOU ANSWERING MY CALLS?" I woke up around 11p and called him back, but he didn't answer. Then, I texted him that I was sleeping. His read receipt was on, so I saw that he read the text. I called him the next day around eight in the morning and he didn't answer. I never heard from him again! I had decided that there had already been too many red flags that I had ignored. Lesson learned, when you see the red flags, leave it alone.

Red is the Color of Warning

Not just at stoplights, but in the pit of your soul.

I saw it flicker in the pauses between his words,

In the way his memory slipped, his story skipped

Like scratched vinyl on old-school love songs.

He brought me roses, sweet as apology,

But petals can't hide thorns

Or bald tires on snow-slick streets,

Or bank accounts with stories that never quite add up.

I let him in, past my threshold and heart,

Filling frames with memories, picturing us whole.

But red shone in heated words over missed calls,

Accusations sharp as winter wind,

His anger insisting I must be guilty for choosing sleep over suspicion.

I bent, apologized for his storms,

Covered cracks with compromise, painted trust over rust.

Still, red puddled at my feet, discomfort in my gut, questions I couldn't shake,

Stories that unraveled when I pulled their threads.

A love that never quite left his living room,

A partnership of privacy and locked phones.

The lesson: when red flags wave,

Don't close your eyes and call them rose petals.

When your spirit whispers "leave," let your feet listen.

I learned love should not bruise, not confuse, not accuse.

And when red flares in your chest, it's not always passion—

When your heart tells you that you deserve better.

Walk away.

Broken Strokes

Being single can get lonely. Because of this I sometimes find myself leaping onto online dating sites to see what's out there. The funny thing about it is that it seems like the same old people that I have seen before, with the same old pictures, doing the same old things are still on sites. It's hard to believe that after five years they are still there. I had met someone, was in a relationship for two years, broke up and got back on the site, yet these same people were still there. But this time it was different. I saw someone out there that caught my eye. Drake was a nice-looking caramel man. His pictures depicted that he was an artist, a painter and that sparked my interest. I love creatives! So, I swiped right. Later on, that day I received a message from him saying that he liked my profile and wanted to chat. So, I obliged him. I usually don't chat long on the dating site because half of the time I do not even remember to go out there to check messages. So, when I do see someone, I may be interested in, I just give them my phone number and tell them to text or call me. I mean when you are in your fifties, you do not have a lot of time to fuck around with all the formalities. Let us just get to know each other and see if this can be anything. He was a 988 counselor. For anyone who doesn't know what that is, it is the "Suicide and Crisis" hotline. That was even more intriguing. So, now I know he is educated, handsome, and creative. To top it off, he lived only 25 minutes away from me. We texted for about an hour that night and decided to talk the next day because he was off work. He worked nights. After a few days of talking on the phone, he asked me if I was interested in meeting him. Of course, I was! I told him to pick the place, and he selected Brown Sugar coffee in Gary, Indiana. It was a quaint new coffee shop. When I googled the pictures and reviews of the place I was impressed. They were black-owned and had wonderful artwork. They also hosted spoken word on some nights. Most of the coffees and teas were African blends.

As I was driving to a parking space I saw a man in the grocery store parking lot next door. He was loading a plethora of groceries into the trunk of this old school, kinda beat up Cadillac. I recalled that on one of Drake's pictures he had on a Cadillac hat. Well, I didn't expect what I saw, but I

rolled with it. He also was a little small in stature. He said he was 5'9 but, it didn't look like it to me. Me of course, really being 5'9 and about 170 lbs. I pay attention to height. I parked and went into Brown Sugar. He came in shortly after I did and was the person I peeped out in the grocery store parking lot. My first thought was "he's kinda tiny." He was smaller than I anticipated and truthfully, I am not turned on by little guys. He certainly was not 5'9. He was more like 5'7.

We were the only two in the shop so there obviously couldn't be any confusion about who each other was. He walked up to me and leaned in for a hug. I obliged. He asked me where I wanted to sit, and I said, "by the fireplace." Although it was June, the ambience was cozy by the fireplace. Soon after we sat down, the owner came over and provided us with a menu. Drake reintroduced himself and promised to bring a piece of artwork for her wall. The conversation was wonderful. We had talked quite a bit on the phone over the last couple of weeks, so I knew some things about him. But what he revealed to me at the coffee shop was even more amazing. Come to find out he was a photographer, a writer and had actually applied for a patent. The other news he wrote to me though was that he was going to Kenya in a few weeks for vacation and business. Apparently, his patent idea required a seamstress to make so he figured he killed two birds with one stone.

On this trip he would be able to find the material that was being purchased for this particular item. This all sounded really good on paper, right? To add he has been divorced for 3.5 years and he was a homeowner. He had been in his home for 3.5 years and finally my favorite thing he was a DJ. The more we talked, we realized that we had so very much in common. I felt comfortable with him. And that small stature started to dissolve because he seemed like he was such a man. After about 2 1/half hours of talking, we parted ways and decided to see each other later that day. I invited him over. For some strange reason, I just didn't feel uncomfortable or unsure or afraid that he might be a Crazy. He came over. We had a few drinks. He loved the view of my backyard and so we sat out there and listen to music. I really enjoyed this company. He left at about 3 o'clock in the morning.

We continued to talk every day. He worked the night so generally by the time I would get home from work he would be up for the day, so our schedule is kind of worked out. What was interesting though, was that he never again invited me out on a date. He spent a lot of time in my house in my backyard. And seeing that he was a night owl from working night most often I would end up falling asleep on him. As a matter of fact, I was just ready to go to bed and leave him downstairs in my living room. He, of course, was quite comfortable.

One day, I decided though, to work from his home. It was my first time going over there. It was a nice cozy place right across the street from a train station. So, I went in and I set up my laptop on the couch next to him. I had a few meetings that I had to attend that day. When I got a break, he gave me a tour of his home. It was a ranch with a basement that was unfinished. He had a lot of his artwork hanging on the walls. I didn't feel uncomfortable at his home, although it was no comparison to mine as it pertains to decor and size. He shared a story about his father, who was a minister. As a spiritualist, I noted this difference between us. During the day, he remarked, "It looks like you came over here to work all day." I thought to myself: "yes, that was the plan.

July 4th was coming, and he wanted to purchase some fireworks. I decided to drive. We went to the fireworks store, he retrieved his items, and we ended up going next-door to get some tacos. While we were in the store, a gentleman walked up to him and spoke. What was strange though is the look that the gentleman gave me. I mean, he looked me up and down. Then he and the young lady he was with left.

At that point, Drake informed me that that was the uncle of a young lady that he had recently dated. On their first date, the young lady had invited him to her son's graduation as a guest. This uncle was the graduation also. And that's how they met. So, the strange look was then understood. The graduation had only taken place about a month earlier. More time went by, and we continued to enjoy each other's company, of course at my house. Then his true self started to show. I almost began to feel badgered by him asking me for sex. We had known each other for about three weeks, and I guess he assumed that sex was on the table. We had stated that we were not going to see anyone else, but I wasn't ready for sex.

At one point we even stopped talking for a couple of days, because of course my answer to his badgering again was "no".

Now I must admit, he was a little sexy. He was very sexy and fine as hell. And the top of all he could kiss. So, I can see how he was a little taken aback because I was really being a tease. That would snuggle up and rub up on that man what his little self. Ok, to be honest, he wasn't that small and stature. Perhaps, I'm exaggerating a little bit. You're being a 5'9 female I kinda like guys over 6 feet. I am clearly gonna wear at least 3 to 4 inches heels and will be looking down at a person that is 5'7, way down. But I must admit, he surprised me one day. I put him to the test. See I got this thing about a man being able to pick me up and hold me up against the wall, if you know what I mean. So, I asked him: "Can you pick me up?" He walked right over to me and picked me up like I was a baby. That goes to show you big in stature doesn't necessarily mean strong. So, I took him up on his request one night and decided to go ahead and put it on him. I knew I was going to do this, but he didn't. A real lady is always prepared. I had taken out some condoms and put them on the nightstand. When he came over, I took him straight to the bedroom. We got undressed and started making out, and I let him know if that point of the condoms were on the nightstand. He gave me the strangest look. It was like he could not believe it. He looked at me like I had a third eye. He uneasily took the condom and put it on. He entered me and pumped one time, and he lost his erection. He had a broken stroke. He went on to tell me that he was disappointed that I had condoms and ask me why I had them. I went on to explain to him. The preparation is everything. I then asked him if he had brought one. And his response was that he had had not. We got into a disagreement, like a big disagreement. I guess at that point he saw me at some type of whore. After that, he politely put his clothes on and left. I talked to him the next day and he wanted to rehash what happened the night before. I clearly did not. I saw absolutely nothing wrong with me having condoms. If you are over 50 years old and have had multiple lovers like I have, I know better than to expect a man to be prepared. If allowed they'll have sex with no condom on with anybody that will allow them to. Guess what though, won't be me. After we got over that little bump, he continued to come over for a little while. Then it happened, he informed me that he was laid off. And his last day would be in two days. In my mind, I'm saying: "Oh here goes this bullshit. Cause, I ain't giving you money for shit. Don't even look my way." I asked him what he was going to do. He said he was going on his trip to Kenya, and he would worry about it when he came back. He said he needed a little time off and that he had stacked some money. He said it would also give him an opportunity to work on his patent. That all sounded great to me. One night he came over and I ran him a bath. Generally, I will go upstairs and sleep while he was still in my living room on the phone watching TV all night. But this night, I decided to lie down in my actual bedroom outside of the bathroom where the tub is located. I have fallen asleep, but I heard him on the phone talking to someone. So of course, seeing I'm laying there, I decided to listen. I could not believe what he was saying. He was on the phone with some lady in Kenya telling her that he loved her. Oh, so now I see what's really going on. I calmly went into the bathroom and sat down on the edge of the tub. He was caught off guard and was trying to rush off the phone. So, I asked him who it was, mind you at 3 o'clock in the morning. He went out to state that it was a travel agent in Kenya that was helping him with his itinerary and transportation when he got there. I went on to ask him: "You always tell your travel agents that you love them?" He responded: "Why are you eavesdropping on my conversation?" At that point, I told him that he could converse with whoever he wanted to at his house. He immediately got out of the tub and put on his clothes. Then he came and sat on the bed where I was attempting to give me a lame excuse in regard to who he was talking to and what that was really about. Of course, I wasn't going. The audacity. The nerve. After our disagreement he left. The next day he called with apologies. I guess he assumed we'd be back to business, as usual. But now I had put him in a special box. The narcissism box. A week went by and we talked on the phone but didn't see each other. At this point it was time for him to go on his Kenya trip. We were talking on the phone one night and I asked him if he was ready for his trip. He said he was, and I did a little research regarding what was needed to enter the country of Kenya. I discovered that he needed an electronic travel authorization and proof of a yellow fever vaccination. Amazingly though, he hadn't gotten either, and he was leaving in two days. Remember the travel agent who was supposed to be helping him with his itinerary and transportation? You know the one he was telling he loved them at 3 o'clock in the morning while he was in my tub. Apparently, she forgot to inform him that he needed these things. Being the helpful person that I am, I forwarded him the information he needed to obtain both. Then I hung up on him and blocked him. More lessons learned. Never let anybody even attempt to make you bad because you are protecting yourself, never hold onto someone too long when you know it's over, and never let a man come over your house and make himself comfortable.

My Home is MY Comfort Not Yours

Let me lay it out, raw on the table—
My mind has been my armor, my shield, my fable.
It has called me forward and said "trust me,"
But my intuition whispers: "protect your peace, always see."
I've learned, never let a man's comfort hijack your home,
never trade wisdom for a wish, nor let your mind roam
Into a space where your value's questioned for being careful,
where condoms become controversy, and honesty is fearful.
If passion isn't matched with respect, it's not yours to lose.
Never let anyone shame your boundaries or your plan, never
mistake a moment's desire for the measure of a man.
I learned to listen when my heart flares red,
To walk away, unashamed, with head held ahead.
Never let someone's lack become your burden or your
debt—
If they're stacked with stories, make sure your soul's not
offset.
Block what hurts, forward what helps, and never feel bad
For protecting your body, your spirit, your pad.
And the biggest lesson, carved firm and deep:
Never let a man make himself at home, while your peace is
his to keep.
Let love be gentle, let boundaries be bold—

Walk away from the story when the lesson's been told.

Perpetual Libations Connoisseur

It was a warm but gloomy day in October in the south suburbs of Chicago, Illinois. I didn't mind the cloudiness because it was 60ish degrees. That made me happy, especially since I was going to my niece Paige's 59th birthday party at a local club, Cooper's. The nurse was caring for my son until 6pm, then my husband was going to relieve her. I put on a lighter jacket and headed to the garage to go. After I parked my car at the venue, a nice black BMW pulled up and parked next to me. The windows were tinted so I couldn't see who was in it. I kindly got out of my car at the almost exact time as the BMW driver and was surprised to see a well-dressed man, seemingly in his 40's. He was wearing a Navy-Blue suit with a tan belt and matching shoes. What struck me the most was that he was also wearing a paisley Ascot and a lapel pin. I thought to myself, I may be a little underdressed. I was wearing a black sweater and some black leather pants. Anyone who knows me knows that I wear all black, all of the time and a lot of accessories. That's my swag.

The gentleman followed behind me and opened the door for me when we reached it. That was when I noticed

that he was about 6 inches shorter than I. He continued his way in the opposite direction. It was the first time that I had been to this venue and it to my surprise it was a nice place and had great energy. After entering I saw some people I recognized, my siblings, so I made my way over to them. We greeted each other and then the birthday girl came up. We were ready to get the festivities started. I went over to the bar and ordered a drink. I must admit that everyone seemed to be having a great time. After a few hours of dancing and enjoying the party, I figured I'd better be getting home. I had a great time, but I was actually a little tired and buzzed. As planned, my husband, Jaden, relieved the nurse, but he had a plethora of questions for me about the party. He could come off jealous sometimes and this one of those times. He asked: "Were guys trying to talk to you? Did you meet someone up there? Who all came?" Just ridiculous. I'll spare you the rest of the details about that marriage as the is a whole other story, but a month later, I filed for divorce.

After I filed for divorce, I found myself frequenting that bar. It was so much that I became a regular. Paige and I would meet there a few times a week and we affectionately named it "The Clubhouse." Our favorite bar star, Mystique, was pouring and we supported her. I mean it as a great time! What was interesting was that the gentleman I met at Paige's birthday party was a regular, as well. I found myself paying a little more attention to him. He would always be alone and would sit in a corner reading a book. He was also always well dressed.

One day in February at the Clubhouse, as he passed by, I introduced myself and he responded: "I'm Karter." I asked him what he was reading, and he told me. He asked me if I read so I opened the books app on my phone and showed him. We had a brief 15-minute conversation that was quite interesting. He told me that he had two sons and lived alone. He said that he was not currently in a relationship, and I shared that I was recently divorced.

Before he left, we exchanged numbers. I texted him a little while later and told him that it was nice talking with him and that I hoped he made it home safely. He responded and said: "I enjoyed the conversation, as well. And yes, I am home safely. Let me know the next time you are going to Cooper's." My thought was: "Why would I let him know the next time I was going to be at "Cooper's? If he wanted to get to know me better, he had my number. Furthermore, that's not an official date, meeting someone at Cooper's." So, I didn't oblige. Funny though, I saw him each time I went to the clubhouse.

When I did, we exchanged pleasantries but never had a conversation again until August. One day, I called Mystique and asked her what she was doing that night? She was not working at The Clubhouse but said she would meet me there.

When I arrived, I chose the seats that Mystique and I would be sitting in as there were only two left at the bar. Then, I got up to order some chicken wings. While ordering Karter came in and sat in one of the seats. Mystique hadn't made it yet and I figured that he would be ordering his drink and going outside as he usually did because he was a smoker. But, to my surprise, he didn't. He sat there and thus we engaged in some great conversation. Next thing I knew, he was telling the other bar star, whatever she wants to drink, put it on my tab. Then entered Mystique. She comes over and speaks to both of us and then says: "Oh, so you didn't save me a seat?" I explained to her that Karter came in and sat down and never left. We laughed as he didn't know that I had been saving the seat for her.

I found myself frequenting the Clubhouse even more. Also, Karter and I began talking on the phone daily, and it was not surprising for us to talk for hours. But what I realized is that he would often call me inebriated and make sexual comments to me. He would say things like: "I want to fuck on you." It disgusted me and I had to let him know. So, I called him one morning and told him that I didn't like it and it probably was not a good idea for us to keep communicating. He said that he felt like it was unfair for me to decide for the both of us nor did I give him the opportunity to change. A few days later, I thought about what he said and called him back. I thought he was a great guy and had a great point. He told me that he was happy I called him and he promised not to do that anymore. We continued to hang out. Karter and I found ourselves drawn together, each time weaving our conversations a little tighter. His demeanor—always poised, always immaculate—masked a vulnerability I only glimpsed when the whiskey glass lingered a bit too long in his hand.

It was not until a rain-soaked Thursday that the mask slipped. The Clubhouse was quiet; there weren't many customers. Karter arrived, his overcoat flecked with droplets, and slid onto the stool beside me. His eyes were more tired than usual, and he ordered a double—no ice, no pretense.

Over the course of the evening, his drinks accumulated, and conversation grew less guarded. He spoke with candor about his struggles. "I feel unseen," he murmured, "…I am always unnoticed." The confession hung between us, intimate and raw, and I felt a empathy toward him that surprised me.

Days passed, and our connection, though complicated by his alcohol dependence, grew stronger. I invited him over one evening, sensing that both of us needed the warmth of company more than ever. He arrived with a flower arrangement almost bigger than he consisting of roses and blood lilly's, my favorite. My home was quiet, scented with lavender and rain, and as the night unfolded, our laughter punctuated the silence, dissolving the boundaries we'd unconsciously maintained.

In the soft glow of lamplight, we found ourselves entwined on my bed, lips tracing familiar territory, hands exploring with gentle urgency. His touch was tentative, as if chasing a memory of desire once easily summoned. But when passion crested and the moment called for surrender, hesitation took hold. Karter's breath grew shallow, and the old anxiety flickered in his eyes. I whispered reassurance, tracing his jawline with my fingertips, letting patience guide me through his discomfort.

He turned away, embarrassed, and confessed with a rueful smile, "There are things whiskey can't fix. Things I wish I didn't have to explain." The frustration was palpable—a vulnerability etched deeper than all his other scars. I drew him close, allowing intimacy to exist in the space between our bodies, not solely in the act itself. The night became about comfort, about learning the language of solace, rather than conquest.

Later, as we lay together in the hush, his hand finding mine beneath the sheets, I realized that connection is not always a steamy conflagration, but sometimes the slow burn of acceptance. We spoke quietly about old wounds; about the way addiction and expectation can make lovers strangers. In the morning, Karter ordered coffee for us both via DoorDash; the ritual, simple and generous, felt like a promise to try again.

Our story did not resolve in one evening. The specter of addiction remained, complicated by the tender ache of disappointment and the hope that intimacy might bloom in unexpected places. We learned to navigate the fragile terrain together, sometimes succeeding, sometimes faltering, but always returning to the bar, the laughter, and the quiet courage of showing up—imperfect, but willing.

Yet as our lives intertwined beyond the soft-lit refuge of my home, Karter's battles with the bottle became harder to overlook. It soon became not uncommon for him to get so drunk at my house that driving himself home was out of the question. I'd usher him to my bedroom and take him out of his clothes. Then he would try something sexual. The smell of liquor from his skin and cigarettes was appalling.

When he was sober enough to attempt sex, he could never reach erection. Then he would fall asleep but his slumber troubled and heavy. He would talk loudly in his sleep and forget I was there. Often hitting me with an elbow. On more than one occasion, I had family gathering and invited him. It was the first time he would be meeting them. He came dressed to the nines. But I was concerned that he would not know when to stop drinking and embarrass himself and me. That time he did not embarrass us, but he did get super drunk and end up staying over. The next invitation to a family event is where things fell completely apart. He had gotten so drunk that he fell asleep at the table, and drooled on himself. He then woke up and poured himself another drink and stood by my sister and best friend. Somehow he his drink over on my sister and the floor. Instead of apologizing and trying to clean up the mess he'd created, he went to the bar and poured himself a refill. Then he sat down on my couch. Soon after, he fell back to sleep, with his mouth wide open and snoring loudly.

This moment stung, embarrassment flashing across my face. After my family left, I locked my bedroom door and slept in the guest room. I knew at some point he would awaken and look for me. He did just as expected around 4am. Once he realized that my bedroom door was locked, he put on his clothes and left. Later on, that morning he called, his usual poise fractured by the memory of slurred exchanges and awkward silences. It was as if his drinking, once a solitary comfort, had begun to spill into the spaces I held dear, challenging not only his dignity but my hope that our story might yet find an easier path.

I knew there was no coming back from that experience and he confirmed it as he went to discuss what happened the night before as he stated: "I don't even want to know what happened." After that we simply didn't talk. The "good morning" texts discontinued. I stopped going to the Clubhouse. I simply did not want the awkwardness.

Finally, I did run into him, and it was I thought, awkward. But I made it easy. We see each other from time to time, but I learned that I must always be cognizant of my deal breakers, and I should never make excuses when they are presented to me.

Be Real with Yourself

Rain-soaked Thursdays, quiet Clubhouse corners

I watched the mask slip, watched tired eyes flicker in lamplight.

Candor pours easily when the glass is full, but truth is bitter on the tongue.

"I feel unseen," he said.

I saw him, saw the ache that chased every swallow.

Thought maybe empathy could be a life raft, maybe laughter could be a shield.

But connection is not conquest.

Not the fevered hush of bodies or the slow burn of hope.

It's learning to hold space when comfort outweighs desire,

To trace jawlines not for longing but for solace.

Whiskey can't mend broken roots.

Some things can't be explained, some things are just there, living loud between the sheets.

I saw love stumble on its own shadow,

Saw addiction spill into sacred spaces—

Family dinners, laughter soured by liquor and sleep.

Embarrassment sharp as a slap, memory fractured, dignity lost among the empty glasses.

Deal breakers knocking at my door—loud, insistent, unforgiving.

So, I learned:

Not every apology fills the cracks.

Not every hope survives the flood.

I locked my bedroom door and slept in another room,

Chose distance over discomfort, silence over excuses.

Watched the "good morning" texts fade to nothing, the Clubhouse lights dim on their own.

We run into each other sometimes, ghosts moving through familiar places.

I make it easy, keep it simple.

Because when deal breakers show up—

You don't invite them in.

You don't build bridges out of broken boundaries.

You stand firm, no excuses.

You choose yourself.

The Best of Times, the Most Toxic of Times – Mr. Midnight

Even thinking about Jules makes me moist still today. I met him on a dating site. His profile picture, him standing next to a white car wearing a white tee and dawning some shades. The smile is what got me though. Damn, he's fine, I thought to myself as I swiped right. No idea that this relationship would thrust me into the most exciting, memorable, and terrifying experience of this lifetime. It impacted me so much that I propelled me onto another timeline.

It wasn't long after I swiped that he reached out to me. We talked through the app for a couple of days before we exchanged phone numbers. And then we started talking on the phone. Next, we became Facebook friends. And about two weeks later, he finally asked to meet me. He told me to pick a place, and I thought that I would be easy on both his pockets and commute. So, I choose TGIF because it was the midway point between his house and mine. I have to say that Jules was honest with me from the beginning. He told me that he was a felon and had been released from prison 3 years prior. My previous male friend was also, and he had seemingly turned himself around, so that didn't scare me. Neither was the fact that his crime was manslaughter. To add, so what he had done 22 years.

Yep, for most women that would be an automatic "hell no." But, not for me. I believe in second chances and that people can evolve and change. Plus, he had sole custody of his daughter Kierra who was 11 years old. He had custody of her since she was 9 after she discovered her mother dead in the bathtub from an overdose of fentanyl. The fact that he had gotten out of prison and immediately fought for his custody wiped away all my fear of his previous life. I thought that was amazing. He lived with his mother and cared for her as well, which also showed compassion and care from my perspective.

I sat in my car and waited for him to arrive instead of going in and getting a table. I was parked in front of the door. I wanted to see him before he saw me. That's an old trick. If he did not look like the guy in the picture I was going to straight drive off. We had not FaceTimed, so I didn't know what I was going to get. I saw a black car circle twice and wondered if it was him. Then a guy walked to the door, and I saw that it was him. He was NOT a catfish. So, I blew my horn and he turned around. I flashed my headlights, and he came over to my car. It was drizzling so I unlocked the passenger door for him to get. He was as handsome as ever. He wore a black peacoat with a black turtleneck sweater. After we were seated and talked, I realized that he felt like home. Before I knew it, we were all but making out, in the restaurant. His kisses were delicious. That date went extremely well! After we ate, he walked me back to my car and I drove him around to his. We talked a little more and he finally got into his car and headed home. Later that night, we talked some more. I liked this guy. He was into astrology, knew how to read the ephemeris, and like talking about it. Days continued to go by, and we talked often about just about everything.

In retrospect though, I realize that the conversation remained the same over the years. We talked about how messed up his mother and daughter were, and how he hated his job. Truthfully, all he had to do was sit in a warm truck and wait to dump some chemicals. I listened patiently to his everyday rant. He never asked about me. The conversations were always about him. I let that go. Perhaps it was loneliness or my desire to be a good woman to a man who had potential. See, I've aways attracted men who needed fixing and Mr. Midnight was no different. After about 2 more weeks I invited him over. I was already in bed, so he joined me. Now this may sound stupid, but I had no intention of having sex with him. But guess what happened. Yes, we did it, we had sex. It was okay, nothing to brag to the girlfriends about, but he certainly seemed to enjoy it. The situationship seemed to take off from there. Jules still had other women that he was talking to, and it was obvious based on the comments they made on his posts.

This of course upset me because I believed that we were further along in our situationship than he did. I got to the point where I got into a full pledge argument with one chick in FaceBook. Instead of setting the record straight with her, he simply got off the app. This was the beginning of the toxicity. Why was I so upset about what he had going on with other women when we never agreed we were monogamous?

Furthermore, why wasn't he choosing me in the way I thought he should? Bottom line was that I was trying to force the relationship. I should have walked away. But, of course, I didn't. I stayed around for the next group of shenanigans. Now he was spending more time with me. He even started bringing his daughter. We pseudo started being a "family". Finally, they officially moved in but we didn't change her school. Once we moved in a lot of things surfaced that were not pleasant. He simply couldn't or wouldn't keep a job. He would work just long enough to catch up on some bills and do some things around the house, then he would get fired and complain about how unfair the company was. He NEVER took accountability for the part he played. We would fight and have sex. He would drink; we would fight and have sex. We both would drink, we would fight and have sex. He would pack up his things and move him and his daughter back to his mom's house. We would break up for a few months, get back together, he would get fired from another job, he would move back in, we would fight, drink, and have sex. This cadence went on for years. I started learning to do things on my own. So, one day I decided to take myself to see the move "Aretha." It was rainy, but I went anyway and really enjoyed myself. Jules called me on the way home and asked me what I was doing. I told him that I had just left the theater and was heading home. He said he was coming over and I welcomed the interaction. When I drove up to my house, I realized that the power was out in the neighborhood. I couldn't get into the garage, so I left my car in the driveway. I went into the house and changed into a night gown. It was around 9pm. About thirty minutes later he knocked on the door. He was wearing a light brown one-piece Carhart. His hood was pulled over his head and he was drenched.

He looked so good. I opened the door and he immediately de-robed having on nothing but his underwear. Oh my God, he was so sexy. I couldn't help myself. He

always drew me back in. The toxicity started all over again. He and his daughter moved back in. He was back to drinking heavily and getting fired from jobs. I was back to checking his phone and location. We were back to drinking and arguing. The sad part about it is that I truly loved him and thought that I could love him along.

By this time, my son was 15 and his daughter Kadiera, was 13. She was going to school in another school system, so I drove her to and from school everyday. She was doing absolutely horribly in school. It was nerve racking as I was the one working with her to help her with her homework. During holiday and summer break, I purchased workbooks so that she did not lose the knowledge she gained during the school year. She hated it and Jules was not supportive. He simply shamed her, thinking that would make her do better. But I realized that there were so many traumas that she was facing, shaming and blaming her was certainly not going to motivate her to better. She was good student when she put her mind to it. So, I knew she was capable. She was depressed, a lot. Jules had simply given up on her. Truthfully, he didn't have the capability or capacity to be a loving father because he had never received support from his mother growing up. Because of this, he ended up becoming a GD (street gang member) and living the street life. I had a suggestion and so did he. Jules had made up in his mind that it would be best for Kadiera to go to job core when she turned 16. I suggested that perhaps that would be the time that my son could possibly go into a long-term facility where he could be cared for 24 hours a day.

We both agreed on the plan for both Kadiera and my son. About three weeks later, we got into a very heated exchange about this three-year plan, and he grabbed me by the neck and pushed me against my car. He accused me of wanting to get rid of the kids so I could live a "hot girl" life and travel without him. He had been drinking and taking his anti-depressant medication and truthfully, I don't know if the interactions between the two substances made him snap or not. I asked him to leave, but he would not. So, I called the police. They showed up four deep along with the firetruck and ambulance. He simply sat in the garage smoking cigarettes and waiting for law enforcement to arrive. When law enforcement arrived, they separated us and asked us about our side of the story individually. The whole encounter was on video because I have a camera in the garage. The incident resulted in him being arrested for domestic violence. Kadiera, immediately got on the phone with her sister Kadrion, who lived about 1.5 hrs away. Her sister came and picked her up. Jules stayed in jail for about a week. In the meantime, I packed all his things and took them to his mother's house. I must admit that I was thoroughly hurt. I thought we were going to make it and I kept Neptuning and making up stories in my head about the relationship being real, caring, and loving. But, that was not the case at all. A few months went by and Jules got a new job with another trucking company. Kadiera was still living with her sister. I missed him horribly. I loved him and being unhealthy was drawn back into the toxicity. One day I reached out to him, and it all started again. Before I knew it, we were back together. But Kadiera didn't move back.

About three years into the relationship, we did something remarkably spontaneous. While sitting in the Costco parking lot, we decided to go and get married. We landed at the courthouse, and I was absolutely enamored that we had chosen each other and was going to make it work. We said our vows and went home. Kadiera was still living with her Kadrion, and we decided that she could come back at the end of the school year. Jules honestly did not want her to come back. Truthfully, neither did I. We seemed to get along better without her. Her birthday passed and during spring break, she decided to visit his mother unbeknownst to him. He was livid! He felt that she was deceitful and only wanted to come back for money, either mine or her grandmother's.

He knew that things were not going well for her living with Kadrion. And truthfully, they were not. Her and her sisters were living from pillar to post as Kadrion's boyfriend was incarcerated and wasn't paying the rent. After the school year ended, with much disdain on our parts, we let Kadiera come home. We were married now, and she was our responsibility. Just as Kadrion picked Kadiera up, she brought her back home. Funny enough, Kadiera came with a guest, her niece, KJ, Kadrion's daughter. Kadrion asked if KJ could spend the summer with us and we allowed it because we figured that they could keep each other company. When Kadrion brought Kadiera back, Jules and I cooked dinner and they ended up spending the night, Kadrion, Konnesha (their other sister) and Kadrion's baby Kadeem, along with KJ. The one night ended up being three nights. That is when we realized that Kadrion and crew were evicted from their new place and had no where to go. She was in the process of trying to determine if she was going to live with her father or try to find a place near us. By day three, I was ready for them to go. Before we knew it, it was fall and time to go back to school. Kadiera was successfully transferred to our school district. Kadrion was still in a bind. So, she asked if KJ could live with us and go to school with Kadiera. We agreed, thinking again that Kadiera and KJ would have each other while navigating a new school.

After a few days of school, we discovered that what we thought was a great idea was not. KJ and Kadiera fought constantly. After about a month, Kadrion had KJ move back with her and I withdrew her from school. I NEVER heard from them again.

After that, things continued to go downhill between Jules and I. The pressure of his drinking and not being able to keep a job, Kadiera hardly doing her homework and getting failing grades, I trying to keep up with my son's needs, I knew this wouldn't last. Then there was the straw that broke the camel's back. Jules cooked dinner one night and decided that he was going to take his brother a plate. He left home around 6pm. At 11pm I called him, he answered and said he was on his way home. By 1am, he still wasn't home. I called and he didn't answer the phone. At 3am, I called again and he answered the phone saying that he was on his way home. By 5am, he still had not made it home, but I had completed divorce papers online. At 7am, I was leaving to pick up my Starbucks coffee, and he pulled into the garage. I told him then that I wanted a divorce. He simply didn't even fight for me. Our divorce was finalized two months later.

The lesson here is to know your worth and don't stay too long. Nothing is worth risking your safety or the safety of your children.

Know Your Worth

There's a light that lives inside you,

Flickering strong, sometimes dimmed by pain.

Love may promise shelter, but storms can gather,

Leaving you battered, standing in the rain.

In the shadow of sweet words,

You lost yourself piece by piece.

Hope became a habit,

And silence your only peace.

But remember, you are golden—

Not meant to rust or break.

Your heart deserves its healing,

Your spirit must awake.

Don't linger in the darkness,

Waiting for love to change its tune.

When hurt becomes the rhythm,

Step away, let go, and soon

You'll find your worth was always there,

Deeper than bruises, stronger than tears.

Choose yourself, walk toward tomorrow,

And leave behind those years.

Shadows at Closing Time

I sat at the far end of the bar, the same spot I'd favored since my divorce five years ago. At 55, I had learned to find comfort in quiet corners, watching the swirl of laughter and flirtation from afar. My heart was tender but wiser, more cautious, less given to reckless hope. I nursed a glass of Cabernet, my gaze drifting over the polished countertop, memories flickering in and out like passing headlights.

I had not expected company that evening, nor did I invite it. But as the hours slipped by and the bar emptied, a man approached. He was neatly dressed, with silver hair and a gentle, self-deprecating smile. "Is this seat taken?" he asked, and the warmth in his voice made her pulse quicken. His name was Charles, sixty and charming, with a knack for weaving stories about old jazz records and European train rides. We talked until closing, both surprised at how easily we shared our quiet histories. I felt the stirrings of something new—hope, or perhaps just the pleasure of being seen.

Our dating began in the shadows. Charles suggested dinners at obscure bistros, little-known art galleries, or long walks in deserted parks. He always chose places where we were unlikely to meet anyone he knew. I noticed, but brushed the thought away—after all, privacy had its appeal. I told herself that I enjoyed the secrecy, that it added intrigue. Yet, when I invited Charles to my favorite café, he declined; when I suggested visiting my home, he hesitated. I never saw his home, never met anyone from his life. Our connection, tender as it was, existed in a world apart, a twilight between truth and longing.

My doubts grew with each stolen evening. The excitement of clandestine meetings soon gave way to unease. I wondered what it meant to live in the shadows of someone else's life—if love could survive in half-light, or if secrecy always demanded a price. I searched for signs, for the slip of a name or an explanation, but Charles was careful. He spoke of work, of music, of memories, but never of the present, never of family. The world he offered me was beautiful, but always just out of reach.

One rainy afternoon, my suspicions found their answer. I saw Charles at the supermarket, his hand entwined with another woman's. I watched as he leaned in close, speaking softly, the intimacy unmistakable. I felt my heart falter, not with anger, but with a sorrow so deep it threatened to drown me. Later, when confronted, Charles admitted the truth: he was married. He cared for me, but he could not offer me a life beyond secrecy—his world was closed, his promises hollow.

In the days that followed, I grieved not the loss of Charles, but the loss of hope. Yet in that pain, I remembered herself—my worth, my strength, the years I had survived and grown. I found comfort in the knowledge that my heart, while bruised, was not broken; I could still choose myself, walk toward tomorrow unafraid. I returned to my favorite spot at the bar, a woman changed, yet still searching for connection. I knew now there were things I would no longer accept: love must stand in the light, and I would never again mistake secrecy for devotion.

My decision was not made out of bitterness, but of self-respect. I understood that healing begins when we see ourselves clearly, when we refuse to linger in darkness waiting for love to change its tune. I watched the world move on around me, and with quiet resolve, stepped into the brightness of my own life, deeper and stronger than before.

Light Beyond the Shadows

In the hush of a dim-lit bar,

She sits alone, her heart scarred but wise,

Nursing memories, swirling in glass,

Watching laughter flicker and rise.

He arrives with a gentle smile,

Stories of jazz and faraway trains,

She lets hope flutter through the door—

A tender pulse, a spark that remains.

But love in twilight always hides

In secret bistros and silent parks,

The world he offers glimmers softly

Yet leaves her longing in the dark.

Until the truth rains quietly down,

His hand in another's, promises thin,

Sorrow, not anger, floods her soul—

She mourns hope, not him.

In grief she recalls her worth,

Chooses herself, stands tall once more,

Vows never again to be cloaked by shadow,

But to seek love where light pours.

The world spins on—she watches, changed,

With quiet strength, she claims her song.

Healing begins when darkness lifts,

And self-respect lights the dawn.

Light in the Gallery

On a gray Saturday afternoon, I wandered through the city's art museum, my footsteps echoing on polished marble floors. At fifty-nine, I had become accustomed to solitary excursions, finding comfort in the quiet contemplation of paintings and sculptures. The vibrant colors and bold brushstrokes reminded me that life, in all its chaos, could still hold beauty. I'd promised myself to remain open to new experiences, even when familiar routines called me back.

Near a luminous installation of blown glass, I noticed a man about my age. He was tall and silver-haired, with bright eyes that lingered on the artwork as if searching for deeper meaning. Our paths crossed by chance, but his warm smile invited conversation.

His name was Daniel—an attractive, well-educated man with a gentle confidence. We spoke of Monet and Chihuly, and I found herself drawn to his intellect, his careful consideration of each piece, and a subtle spirituality that colored his observations.

Over coffee in the museum café, Daniel shared stories of his twin daughters and his joy in cooking their favorite meals. He spoke of his digital content company, explaining how he used creativity and technology to connect people with inspiring stories. I listened, captivated by his passion and the way he described balancing business with fatherhood. I admired his grounded presence and the ease with which he moved through the world, as if he'd come to know himself deeply.

Our conversations grew more frequent and meaningful. I found herself looking forward to each encounter, savoring the intellectual banter and gentle laughter. I felt a sense of renewal—a flutter of anticipation I hadn't experienced in years. Daniel's spirituality resonated with me, and his openness about life's struggles made me trust him more. In moments of silence, I wondered if I might be ready to let someone in again.

One evening, as we walked among the museum's contemporary pieces, Daniel's voice grew quieter. He confessed he was in recovery for drug addiction, attending regular NA meetings to maintain his sobriety. I listened, my heart tensing with concern and empathy. He explained how the community had become a lifeline—friends who understood his journey, women and men whose stories mirrored his own.

But as days passed, I learned that Daniel's recovery was not without complication. Through gentle honesty, he admitted being romantically involved with several women from his NA meetings. The revelation struck me unexpectedly, stirring a mixture of disappointment, understanding, and self-reflection.

In the days that followed, I sat with my feelings, allowing sorrow and confusion to wash over me. I questioned my readiness for vulnerability and wondered if hope for romance was naïve at my age.

Yet, as she strolled the museum's quiet halls once more, I recalled my own worth. I recognized that Daniel's journey was his own, and his choices did not diminish my value.

I resolved to seek love where honesty and light prevailed. I would not allow shadows of another's secrets to obscure her path. With renewed clarity, I cherished the connection we'd shared but chose to move forward, my heart open yet anchored by self-respect.

In the soft glow of the gallery, I understood that healing began when I honored herself—and that sometimes, the greatest art was the act of claiming my own song.

Gallery of Light

In marble halls where echoes roam,

A solitary heart finds gentle space.

She wanders past glass and painted dream,

Seeking color in the world's embrace.

A silver-haired stranger stands in light,

His eyes, a gallery of searching grace.

In shared laughter and thoughtful gaze,

She rediscovers the courage to face.

Stories poured like coffee's steam—

Of daughters, meals, and digital art.

Trust blooms, fragile and new,

A hesitant hope within her heart.

But shadows linger, softly cast,

Revelations spoken in a hush.

A tangle of love and honesty,

The ache of promise, the sting of trust.

She grieves, she wonders, she quietly aches,

In silent halls where sorrows swell.

Yet in her soul, a dawn unfolds—

A tender light she knows so well.

She claims her worth in golden rays,

Letting go with gentle, open hands.

For healing starts where self is honored,

And in her heart, her own song stands.

The Dawn

At fifty-nine, I had grown used to the echoes of my own footsteps against the hardwood floors of my neat, sunlit home. Sometimes, the stillness felt like a gentle silence; other days, it pressed down like a heavy blanket. my son had been the center of my world for so long—now he was nineteen. I was proud of my independence and accomplishments, but with each passing birthday, I felt the contours of my loneliness more acutely.

I filled my days with familiar comforts: Sunday brunches with my sorority sisters, who became family after my divorce; book club meetings sprinkled with laughter; and, when night fell, hours spent curled on my velvet couch, letting Netflix series blur into one another. The banter on the screen often felt like the only conversation in my house. Yet beneath it all, a yearning for companionship—something real, raw, and close—quietly pulsed.

One evening, as golden twilight crept through my curtains, I lingered over my tea, thumb circling the rim of my mug. I wondered out loud—just for a moment—if life could offer me another chance at a deep connection. The idea of online dating had always seemed intimidating, but with my friends' gentle encouragement and a nudge from within, I found myself scrolling through profiles, heart fluttering with nervous hope.

My profile was honest: "Retired HR Leader, proud mother of a wonderful special needs son, lover of music and early morning walks, looking for laughter and a good conversation." Within a week, my inbox pinged with messages, but only one caught my attention. Cedric—"Ced," he introduced himself—was a fifty-two-year-old with a cropped silver beard, striking gray-green eyes, and a mischievous smile.

Our first messages were light and playful. I learned Ced was a stepper, active in his fraternity, and a champion bid whist player. He cooked Sunday dinners for his niece and called himself a "family guy through and through." We shared love of R&B music and playing cards set an easy rhythm to our digital conversations. Soon, Ced invited me to a jazz club for our first in-person meeting.

That night, nerves fluttered in my stomach as I slipped on her favorite black suit and dabbed on some Creed parfum. Ced arrived with a bouquet of sunflowers and a warmth that made me feel seen. He was attentive, quick-witted, and his laughter filled the empty corners in my spirit. Over the following weeks, our connection deepened. We danced at fraternity socials, cooked together on Sunday afternoons, and wandered through the park, hand in hand. I found myself opening up in ways I hadn't in years, trusting Ced with stories I'd once kept guarded.

For a while, the ache of loneliness faded into joy. Ced's presence felt like the dawn after a long night. Friends noticed my lighter step and brighter smile. I felt cherished, desired, and, most of all, hopeful about this new chapter.

Yet, as the weeks turned to months, small things began to unsettle me. Ced was fiercely protective of his phone, sometimes distant after certain calls. He canceled last-minute, citing work or family obligations. I told herself not to overthink—after all, everyone had their secrets, and trust was built over time.

One Saturday afternoon, I decided to surprise Ced at a bustling riverside café, hoping to brighten his day. He told me that he was going to have an early lunch there as it was one of his favorite places to eat. I stepped inside and spotted him immediately—his unmistakable stature, the way he gestured animatedly while talking. But it was his companion that made my heart freeze: a handsome man, laughter dancing between them, Ced's hand resting lightly on the man's knee.

Shock surged through me as the truth revealed itself in a glance—Ced was not only drawn to me. The world seemed to tilt, memories of late-night talks, shared dreams, and Ced's steady presence swirling into confusion. I left quietly, my chest tight and my thoughts a tangle of hurt and betrayal. For days, I replayed every conversation, searching for clues, wondering if I had missed something.

When Ced called, voice thick with apology, he confessed his truth: he was bisexual, a part of himself he kept hidden out of fear and habit. He insisted his feelings for me were genuine, but the secret lingered between us, changing the light in which I saw him—and myself.

I grieved not only for the romance lost but for the trust shaken. Yet, as the hours turned to days, I turned inward, allowing myself to feel the sting of disappointment but refusing to let it define me. I understood, perhaps for the first time, that my loneliness did not make me unworthy, nor was my joy dependent on another's truth.

With time, I found strength in my resilience. I spent more evenings with her sisters, laughed until my sides ached, and returned to the comfort of my stories—both on the page and on the screen. I reconnected with old friends, sharing more than smiles and small talk, inviting them into my journey of healing and self-discovery.

In letting go—with gentle, open hands—I honored her own heart, allowing space for new beginnings. The ache of loneliness softened, replaced by a newfound sense of self-worth and possibility. I walked forward, hopeful, carrying the dawn within me.

Healing

A Poem Inspired by Resilience

In the hush that follows heartbreak's shatter,

I gathered the pieces—soft, trembling, sure—

Each shard a memory, laughter or ache,

Each glimmer a step toward becoming more.

I learned to cradle the sting of loss gently,

To honor grief without letting it stay,

For inside the ache of trust undone,

I found the dawn that opens each day.

Sisters' laughter became my healing balm,

Old friends' voices, a bridge to who I'd been.

In stories, in song, in evenings aglow,

I rediscovered my spirit within.

Letting go with hands uncurled and kind,

I honored the heart that still hopes, still yearns.

Not unworthy, not defined by longing,

But walking forward with each lesson learned.

Now, loneliness softens, courage grows near,

The light I carry is wholly my own.

In the healing found after heartbreak's end,

I rise—resilient, radiant, grown.

www.ingramcontent.com/pod-product-compliance
Lightning Source LLC
LaVergne TN
LVHW052255100826
845147LV00001B/54

* 9 7 9 8 9 9 9 4 2 3 1 0 8 *